Copyright © 2011 XAMonline, Inc.
All rights reserved. No part of the material protected by this copyright notice may be reproduced or utilized in any form or by any means, electronic or mechanical, including photocopying, recording or by any information storage and retrievable system, without written permission from the copyright holder.

To obtain permission(s) to use the material from this work for any purpose including workshops or seminars, please submit a written request to:

XAMonline, Inc.
25 First Street, Suite 106
Cambridge, MA 02141
Toll Free: 1-800-509-4128
Email: info@xamonline.com
Web: www.xamonline.com
Fax: 1-617-583-5552

Library of Congress Cataloging-in-Publication Data

Wynne, Sharon A.
    MTEL English as a Second Language (ESL) 54 Practice Test 1: Teacher Certification / Sharon A. Wynne. -1st ed.
    ISBN: 978-1-60787-320-4
    1. MTEL English as a Second Language (ESL) 54 Practice Test 1 2. Study Guides
    3. MTEL   4. Teachers' Certification & Licensure   5. Careers

Disclaimer:
The opinions expressed in this publication are the sole works of XAMonline and were created independently from the National Education Association, Educational Testing Service, or any State Department of Education, National Evaluation Systems or other testing affiliates.

Between the time of publication and printing, state specific standards as well as testing formats and website information may change that is not included in part or in whole within this product. Sample test questions are developed by XAMonline and reflect similar content as on real tests; however, they are not former tests. XAMonline assembles content that aligns with state standards but makes no claims nor guarantees teacher candidates a passing score. Numerical scores are determined by testing companies such as NES or ETS and then are compared with individual state standards. A passing score varies from state to state.

Printed in the United States of America   œ-1
MTEL English as a Second Language (ESL) 54 Practice Test 1
ISBN: 978-1-60787-320-4

MTEL ENGLISH AS A SECOND LANGUAGE (ESL) 54 PRACTICE TEST 1

LISTENING SECTION: ORAL GRAMMAR AND VOCABULARY

Directions: In this part of the actual test, you will hear and read a series of short speeches of nonnative speakers of English. Then you will be asked questions about each student's problems in grammar or vocabulary in the recorded speech. You will be allotted ample time to answer the questions.

1. Listen to an ESOL student talk about his experience with working in the United States.
(Average)

   (Taped excerpt)

   I'm studying Business Administration. I was in the second semester.

   The verb *was* in the second sentence is incorrect with respect to:

   A. Tense
   B. Gender
   C. Person
   D. Number

2. Listen to an ESOL student talking about her mother's food.
(Easy)

   (Taped excerpt)

   My mom's cooking is too good.

   The adverb *too* is incorrect with regards to:

   A. Usage
   B. Form
   C. Spelling
   D. Word order

3. Listen to an ESOL student talking about a math grade he received.
(Easy)

   (Taped excerpt)

   Just look at this math grade from my teacher. He says I was missing an explanation of my answer.

   The verb *was missing* is incorrect with regard to:

   A. Tense
   B. Agreement
   C. Subjunctive
   D. Number

4. **Listen to an ESOL student talking about her pet bird.**
(Average)

(Taped excerpt)

This bird causes much problems every day.

The word *much* is incorrect with regard to the use of _____ nouns.

A. count/no count
B. regular/irregular
C. collective
D. compound

5. **Listen to an ESOL student talking about having children.**
(Rigorous)

(Taped excerpt)

Many people are afraid of having and to raise children.

The words *to raise* are incorrect with regard to:

A. Tense
B. Agreement
C. Parallel structure
D. Adverbial format

6. **Listen to an ESOL student talking to her friend about her beliefs on conducting relationships with others.**
(Rigorous)

(Taped excerpt)

How one behaves towards others is more important than anything else.

One refers to:

A. You
B. They
C. The listener
D. The speaker

7. **Listen to an ESOL student talking about Faulkner's novels.**
(Average)

(Taped excerpt)

Faulkner's books are interesting novels. They are difficult to understand, but it illustrate life in the South.

The word *it* is incorrect with respect to:

A. Reference
B. Number
C. Gender
D. Class

ESOL PRACTICE TEST

8. **Listen to an ESOL student talking to her friend about life in the United States.**
(Average)

(Taped excerpt)

I have no stomach for pork.

The word *stomach* means:

A. Enlarged storage cavity, in invertebrates
B. A digestive organ
C. The abdomen or belly
D. Appetite for food

9. **Listen to an ESOL student talking about her sister's beliefs on eternal love.**
(Easy)

(Taped excerpt)

My sister talks about love all the time. As far as I can see, she makes no sense. Her arguments have neither rhyme or reason.

The word *or* in the last sentence is incorrect with regard to:

A. Parallel structure
B. Usage
C. Form
D. Person

10. **Listen to an ESOL student talking about her father.**
(Easy)

(Taped excerpt)

My father's name is Jonathan. He was named for her great grandfather.

The word *her* is incorrect with regard to:

A. Agreement
B. Gender
C. Person
D. Number

LISTENING: PRONOUNCIATION

Directions: In this part of the actual test, you will hear and read a series of short speeches of nonnative speakers of English. Then you will be asked questions about each student's problems in pronunciation in the recorded speech. You will not be asked to evaluate the student's grammar or vocabulary usage. To help you answer the questions, the speech will be played a second time. You will be allotted ample time to answer the questions.

11. Listen to an ESOL student reading aloud the following sentence.
    (Rigorous)

    (Taped excerpt)

    The TV program was live. (Student pronounces *live* as [lɪv].

    The error in pronunciation in the word *live* indicates a problem with:

    A. Diphthongs
    B. Primary cardinal vowels
    C. Triphthongs
    D. Allophones

12. Listen to an ESOL student reading aloud the following sentence.
    (Rigorous)

    (Taped excerpt)

    Please bring me a hamburger and some fries. (Student pronounces *and* as [aend].)

    The error in pronunciation in the word *and* indicates a problem with:

    A. Elision
    B. Assimilation
    C. Phonemes
    D. Weakness

13. Listen to an ESOL student reading aloud the following sentence.
    (Rigorous)

    (Taped excerpt)

    I am the chairman of the debate club. (Student pronounces *chairman* as [sheərmən].)

    The error in pronunciation of the word *chairman* indicates problems with:

    A. Affricatives
    B. Plosives
    C. Laterals
    D. Glides

14. Listen to an ESOL student reading aloud the following sentence.
(Average)

(Taped excerpt)

I believe that my class is starting. (Student pronounces *my* as [mi].

The error in pronunciation of the word *my* indicates problems with:

A. Short vowels
B. Diphthongs
C. Triphthongs
D. Long vowels

15. Listen to an ESOL student reading aloud the following sentence.
(Average)

(Taped excerpt)

What are you reading? (Student pronounces *are* as [är].)

The error in pronunciation of the word *are* indicates problems with:

A. Schwa
B. Stress
C. Suprasegmentals
D. Prosody

16. Listen to an ESOL student reading aloud the following sentence.
(Rigorous)

(Taped excerpt)

I would like a thin slice of cheesecake. (Student pronounces *thin* as [ðin].)

The error in pronunciation of the word *thin* indicates problems with:

A. Labials
B. Affricatives
C. Palatals
D. Fricatives

17. Listen to an ESOL student reading aloud the following sentence.
(Rigorous)

(Taped excerpt)

I want to be a marine scientist. (Student pronounces *want to be* as [want to be].)

The error in pronunciation of the words *want to be* indicates problems with:

A. Fricatives
B. Assimilation
C. Linking
D. Elision

ESOL PRACTICE TEST

18. Listen to an ESOL student reading aloud the following sentence.
(Average)

(Taped excerpt)

I saw *The King's Speech* last night. (Student pronounces and emphasizes each word.)

The error in speaking the sentence indicates problems with:

A. Intonation
B. Linking sounds
C. Pitch
D. Stress-timing

19. Listen to an ESOL student reading aloud the following sentence.
(Average)

(Taped excerpt)

The band has just signed with a new record label. (Student pronounces *record* as [re/CORD].)

The error in pronunciation of the word *record* indicates problems with:

A. Pitch
B. Reduction
C. Stress
D. Rhythm

20. Listen to an ESOL student reading aloud the following sentence.
(Rigorous)

(Taped excerpt)

What do you plan to do after graduation? (Student pronounces *graduation* with a rising voice.)

The error in pronunciation of the word *graduation* indicates problems with:

A. Pitch
B. Stress
C. Function words
D. Intonation

FOUNDATIONS OF LINGUISTICS AND LANGUAGE LEARNING

Directions: In this part of the test, you will read a series of short writing samples produced by nonnative speakers of English. You will be asked to identify the errors in the students' writing. Therefore, before taking the test, you should be familiar with the writing of nonnative speakers who are learning English.

Questions 21-23 are based on the following excerpt from an essay describing a popular sport in the student's native country.

> *Soccer of my country is a very popular sport in every city. Soccer players must has skill kicking the ball. They train every day so that he can become superstars.*

21. In the first sentence, the error is in the relative order of:
    (Average)

    A. A noun and an adjective
    B. The direct and indirect objects
    C. The subject and object
    D. The prepositional phrases

22. The second sentence contains an error in the:
    (Average)

    A. Agreement between the pronoun and verb
    B. Pronoun antecedent and referent
    C. Structure of the subordinate clause
    D. Order of the sentence elements

23. The last sentence contains an error in the:
    (Average)

    A. Noun and an adjective
    B. Direct and indirect objects
    C. Subject and the object
    D. Pronoun form

Questions 24-26 are based on an excerpt from an essay describing the student's favorite foods.

> *My favorite food for breakfast is a cup of hot chocolate with a bread and a piece of cheese. In my country we eat a lot of beef and beans. There are always any beans for every meal. There is also rice at every meal too. Visitors in my country likes to eat fruit or arequipe for dessert.*

24. In the first sentence, there is an error in the:
    (Average)

    A. Verb tense
    B. Parallel structure
    C. Punctuation
    D. Subject and object

25. In the third sentence, the word *any* is incorrect because:
    (Rigorous)

    A. *Some* is used with count nouns
    B. *Any* is used with noncount nouns
    C. *Any* is used in questions
    D. *Any* is used in negative statements

26. In sentence 5, the correct form of the verb *likes* should be:
    (Average)

    A. like
    B. liked
    C. will like
    D. have liked

Directions: Each of the questions or statements that follow is followed by four possible answers or completions. Select the one that is best in each of the remaining questions.

27. *Eight* and *ate* are examples of which phonographemic differences?
    (Average)

    A. Homonyms
    B. Homographs
    C. Homophones
    D. Heteronyms

28. *Bow (to bend)*, *bow (front part of a ship)*, and *bow (a decorative knot)* are examples of which phonographemic differences?
    (Easy)

    A. Homonyms
    B. Homographs
    C. Homophones
    D. Heteronyms

29. In the statement *Fido got bitten by a huge snake*, the stress would fall on which word?
    (Easy)

    A. Fido
    B. got bitten
    C. huge
    D. snake

30. In *morphemic analysis*, you need to study:
    (Easy)

    A. The smallest unit within a language system to which meaning is attached
    B. The way in which speech sounds form patterns
    C. The way the word is spelled
    D. The root word and the suffix and/or prefix

31. The study of *morphemes* helps the student understand:
    (Average)

    A. How to sound out a word
    B. Diphthongs
    C. Grammatical information
    D. Predicates

ESOL PRACTICE TEST

32. If you are studying *semantics*, then you are studying:
(Easy)

    A. Intonation and accent when conveying a message
    B. Culture
    C. The definition of individual words and meanings
    D. The subject-verb-object order of the English sentence

33. Which one of the following is *not* included in the study of syntax?
(Average)

    A. The parts of speech
    B. The parts of a sentence
    C. Inflections of different words
    D. Sentence transformations

34. In the following sentence: "I had a few nuts before my meal" which word is an example of a countable, common noun?
(Easy)

    A. I
    B. had
    C. few
    D. nuts

35. To which subcategory of subordinating conjunction does *as soon as* belong?
(Average)

    A. Time
    B. Cause and effect
    C. Contrast
    D. Condition

36. Which kind of sentence is the following sentence: "When the tornado was near, the sky darkened and the wind grew stronger."
(Average)

    A. Simple sentence
    B. Compound sentence
    C. Complex sentence
    D. Compound-complex sentence

37. To change the active voice sentence "The poet read the poem" to a passive voice sentence, the correct form would be:
(Easy)

    A. The poem read the poet.
    B. The poem is being read by the poet.
    C. The poem is read by the poet.
    D. The poem was read by the poet.

38. When a teacher says: "Please sit down" she is trying to get the students to do something. This is an example of:
(Easy)

   A. Synonyms
   B. Speech acts
   C. Culture in the classroom
   D. Body language

39. When someone warns "Don't miss the boat", the speaker is using a/an:
(Easy)

   A. Cognate
   B. Derivational morpheme
   C. Phrase
   D. Idiom

40. The French word "bleu" and the English word "blue" are examples of:
(Easy)

   A. Heteronyms
   B. Transformations
   C. Idioms
   D. Cognates

41. What has been the most important factor in the growth of English?
(Easy)

   A. The invasion of the Germanic tribes in England
   B. The pronunciation changes in Middle English
   C. The extension of the British Empire
   D. The introduction of new words from different cultures

42. When people in the same profession use language to communicate, they frequently use _____ to communicate their thoughts.
(Easy)

   A. code switching
   B. cognates
   C. elaborated code
   D. jargon

43. If you are studying *disglossia*, then you are studying:
(Easy)

   A. The definition of individual words and meanings
   B. How context impacts the interpretation of language
   C. Meaning that is stored or inherent, as well as contextual
   D. The use of separate dialects to the use of separate languages

ESOL PRACTICE TEST

44. Register refers to the language used depending on:
(Average)

A. The relationship between the speakers
B. The communicative competence of the speakers
C. The polite discourse involved
D. The culture of the speakers

45. In analyzing World Englishes, Kachru classified countries as members of:
(Rigorous)

A. Former colonies and colonialists
B. First world and third world countries
C. Dominate cultures and subordinate cultures
D. Inner, outer, and expanding circles

46. English as it is spoken around the world is referred to as _____.
(Average)

A. the Queen's English
B. world English
C. substandard English
D. Standard American English

47. Skinner's "operant conditioning" was based upon his belief that language was learned by:
(Average)

A. Interaction with their environment
B. New knowledge must be reconciled with old
C. Stimulus-response actions
D. A language acquisition device

48. In Gattegno's *Silent Way*, students:
(Average)

A. Repeat the phrases spoken by the teacher
B. Carefully study charts, gestures, and hints from the teacher
C. The students must remain silent
D. The instructor uses abundance speech to teach the sound system

49. A teacher who instructs students to "Open the door" or "Go to the whiteboard" is using which basic language approach/method?
(Average)

A. The Silent Way
B. Notional/functional
C. Total Physical Response (TPR)
D. Natural Approach

50. **By learning lexical chunks, English language learners (ELLs) develop:**
(Average)

   A. Lexis
   B. Fluency
   C. Jargon
   D. Private speech

51. **Prabhu was most closely associated with which methodology?**
(Rigorous)

   A. Subordinate teaching to learning
   B. Notional/functional syllabus
   C. Delayed oral response
   D. Reasoning and problem solving

52. **A second-language learner who is in the formulaic speech level is in which stage of development?**
(Rigorous)

   A. Knows 500 receptive words
   B. Knows 1000 receptive words
   C. Knows 3000 receptive words
   D. Knows 6000 receptive words

53. **Syntax is acquired by second-language learners:**
(Average)

   A. At the same rate in L1 and L2
   B. Faster in L2 than L1
   C. In the same order as L1
   D. In different order than L1

54. **Code-switching refers to the ability of the speaker to:**
(Rigorous)

   A. Use dialect appropriately
   B. Develop an inter-language
   C. Switch languages to express oneself
   D. Use empty speech

55. **Which of the following is a strategy of language-learners?**
(Easy)

   A. Communicative competence
   B. Bilingualism
   C. Interlanguage
   D. Interference

56. **The inability of a language student to conjugate verb forms is probably an example of:**
(Easy)

   A. Private speech
   B. Cognitive factors that affect speech
   C. Interference
   D. Fossilization

ESOL PRACTICE TEST

57. **Which of the following is an example of a language learner having problems with simplification?**
(Easy)

    A. Occurs when the learner adds -ed to all verbs
    B. Might say "I like sky the blue."
    C. Hispanics pronouncing words like *student* as *estudent*
    D. Asking someone if "You like?" instead of "Do you like this one?"

58. **According to Krashen, English language learners acquire which of the following language structures last?**
(Rigorous)

    A. Auxiliary verb, article
    B. Irregular past tense verbs
    C. –ing, copula
    D. Possessives

59. **Which of the following is an example of intrinsic motivation in relation to language learning?**
(Average)

    A. A need based on job requirements
    B. A parental imposition on a child
    C. A need caused by living in a bilingual community
    D. A desire to know another culture more intimately

60. **What type of scaffolding is the teacher demonstrating when she places students together in work groups?**
(Rigorous)

    A. Interactive
    B. Shared
    C. Modeling
    D. Independent

61. **Which one of the following is an effective question in a guided scaffolding activity?**
(Average)

    A. Can you tell me the purpose of this activity?
    B. What is the name of this plant?
    C. Which one of you started the clock?
    D. Do you remember last week when we classified other plants?

62. **According to Krashen and Terrell's *Acquisition Hypothesis*, language learning is:**
(Average)

    A. Subconscious learning and conscious learning
    B. Formal study
    C. An invariable path
    D. Comprehensible input

63. The researcher most closely associated with communicative competence is:
    (Easy)

    A. Bernstein
    B. Fishman
    C. Hymes
    D. Labov

64. Though there are exceptions, the most common purposes of a narrative are to:
    (Rigorous)

    A. Tell a story or incident, explain a process, or explain cause and effect
    B. Inform people or persuade them to act or think differently about a topic
    C. Used to stimulate the senses which support the text or create spatial in a text
    D. Divide, define, or compare and contrast

65. In a top-down strategy of literacy development, which one of the following undesirable strategies might a reader use?
    (Average)

    A. Read words
    B. Read phrases
    C. Ignore title and typeface
    D. Achieves general understanding

66. According to Ehri's continuum of word reading development, which one of the following belongs to the mature alphabetic phase of the alphabetic principle?
    (Rigorous)

    A. Tries to remember words by incidental visual characteristics
    B. Relies on letter names to identify words
    C. Can represent almost every sound with a logical letter choice
    D. Remembers multisyllabic words

67. According to Collier, parents should *not* use a second language in the home because:
    (Rigorous)

    A. They will make many mistakes
    B. They may experience difficulties in expressing themselves
    C. They are working below their actual cognitive level
    D. Their children receive sufficient L2 instruction in their schools

68. Which of the following options is considered to be a reason for continuing to develop L1 literacy with English Language Learners (ELLs)?
 (Average)

    A. L2 literacy is achieved quicker
    B. Subtle L2 pragmatics can be understood better
    C. More mature cognitive development is achieved
    D. Learning L2 vocabulary is easier

69. The direct method involves:
 (Average)

    A. Commands that students must carry out
    B. The use of vivid pictures and choices
    C. Use of oral language and grammar learned inductively
    D. A story is dictated to be practice read

70. Which of the following is *not* a benefit of storytelling according to Wajnryb?
 (Average)

    A. It appeals to the affective domain
    B. It reduces anxiety by forging listening experience
    C. It is pedagogically positive
    D. It is artificial communication

71. Which of the following models' goal is bilingualism?
 (Easy)

    A. Indigenous language immersion
    B. Pull-out ESL
    C. SDAIE
    D. Transition

72. In student-centered learning the teacher's role is that of a _____?
 (Rigorous)

    A. guide
    B. cheerleader
    C. facilitator
    D. coach

73. In teaching English Language Learners, which of the following is a valid reason for using peer tutoring?
 (Average)

    A. To relieve tension
    B. To reinforce learning in the tutor
    C. To allow students to learn in a different mode
    D. To practice English at will

74. Which of the following reasons is an advantage to using machines in the ESOL classroom?
 (Average)

    A. They are inexpensive
    B. They are nonjudgmental
    C. They are fun
    D. They are better than teachers

75. Which one of the following teaching practices is *not* a valid listening comprehension strategy?
    (Rigorous)

    A. Listening for discourse markers
    B. Use of good reading texts
    C. Using repetition and facial expressions
    D. Summarizing and retelling stories

76. Why would the average Spanish speaking ELL need extra work on the English vowels?
    (Average)

    A. English vowels are different from L1 of the Spanish speaker
    B. There is no sound-symbol correspondence in the English vowels
    C. Spelling of English vowels and their sounds is easy
    D. English has multiple vowel sounds

77. Which one of the following is *not* a strategy used in content-based learning?
    (Rigorous)

    A. Accessing prior knowledge
    B. Modifying state-mandated, content-area textbooks
    C. Providing comprehensible feedback
    D. Allowing 10 minutes free-reading time after recess

78. Which one of the following is *not* a metacognitive learning strategy?
    (Average)

    A. Review a key concept
    B. Skim for information
    C. Create optimal learning conditions
    D. Keeping track of errors

79. Which researcher(s) is(are) most closely associated with the schema theory?
    (Average)

    A. Rossell & Baker
    B. Gersten
    C. Carrell & Eisterhold
    D. Lambert

80. Incorporating prior knowledge into L2 learning permits ELLs to:
    (Average)

    A. Permits readers to learn and remember less
    B. Improves reading comprehension
    C. Avoids in-depth study
    D. Stimulates a lack of comprehension

81. Which of the following instructional strategies would promote fluency?
    (Average)

    A. Playing vocabulary games
    B. Explicit study of vocabulary lists
    C. Role plays
    D. Using computer language games

82. **According to many, the easiest single strategy for remembering new vocabulary is:**
    (Average)

    A. Names placed on classroom objects
    B. Learning new words from special lists
    C. TPR activities
    D. Singing

83. **Which of the following reasons is a valid reason for providing different material on the same subject to a classroom of ELL students?**
    (Average)

    A. It's easier than summarizing all the material
    B. Different textbooks cover different aspects of the subject
    C. Students need to fill in their Know-Want-Learn charts by reading a lot
    D. No two people learn alike

84. **Realia often is used in classrooms. Which one of the following would be a valid example of realia for teaching about genetics?**
    (Average)

    A. A set of different colored gemstones
    B. A balance scale
    C. Gerbils of different colors
    D. A pizza

85. **One reason young children are often considered better language learners than older children or an adult is children:**
    (Rigorous)

    A. Are more emotionally open to learning a new language
    B. Have more access to comprehensible input
    C. Are able to use inductive reasoning
    D. Are tied to their native language and culture

86. **Which of the learning tendencies (Reid, 1987) most accurately describes a student who enjoys doing lab experiments?**
    (Rigorous)

    A. Visual
    B. Auditory
    C. Kinesthetic
    D. Tactile

87. **Which of the following is the most common method for determining if an ELL has possible learning disabilities?**
    (Rigorous)

    A. Observation and interpretation
    B. A language diagnostic test
    C. Documentation of at least 1 intervention
    D. Consultation with the principal about ELL's progress

88. Which of the following is an example of distortion in pronunciation?
(Rigorous)

   A. Pronouncing lake as cake
   B. Pronouncing ship as chip
   C. Pronouncing liked as like-id
   D. Dropping of the final consonants of words

89. An ELL suspected of being gifted might demonstrate which of the following behaviors?
(Rigorous)

   A. May present behavioral problems when asked to produce written work
   B. Has the ability to decode successfully but difficulty in comprehensions
   C. Should be analyzed for up to 10 weeks using ESOL techniques
   D. May demonstrate the ability to solve problems not dependent on English

90. Which one of the following features is *not* a key feature of group learning projects?
(Average)

   A. Ability groups for regular daily tasks
   B. Monitoring group work during the task
   C. Assessing both individual and group achievements
   D. Meaningful tasks

91. When the teacher is correcting a student's language, the teacher should:
(Easy)

   A. Carefully correct all mistakes
   B. Consider the context of the error
   C. Ignore the error and increase correct input
   D. Correct only those errors that interfere with meaning

92. Which one of the following is a purpose of feedback?
(Rigorous)

   A. To model structures correctly
   B. To correct mistakes
   C. To illustrate alternative forms of speech
   D. To provide assessment and correction

93. Which of the following strategies will help develop vocabulary in a non-threatening way?
(Rigorous)

   A. Menus from local restaurants
   B. Word lists for the upcoming readings
   C. Activate prior knowledge about the content, especially vocabulary
   D. Explicit instruction in the content vocabulary

94. Which of the following activities is the most effective in learning to self-edit a written text?
    (Rigorous)

    A. Checking the text for spelling errors
    B. Checking the text for grammatical errors
    C. Using a checklist provided by the teacher
    D. Revising word order

95. Which of the following tests is used to evaluate foreign students entering the university?
    (Rigorous)

    A. CELDT
    B. BEAR
    C. Iowa Test of Basic Skills
    D. TOEFL

96. Which of the following provides extra help to disadvantaged students in math and reading?
    (Rigorous)

    A. No Child Left Behind
    B. The Dream Act
    C. Race to the Top
    D. Title I

97. Which one of the following is *not* an alternative assessment strategy used to back up oral placement testing results?
    (Rigorous)

    A. Teacher observation
    B. Conferencing
    C. Oral interviews
    D. Interviews

98. Which of the following alternative assessment strategies is used to promote an inner dialogue for ELLs?
    (Average)

    A. Portfolios
    B. Observation
    C. Self-assessment
    D. Journals

99. Which of the following accommodations may be allowed for ELLs with less than one year in the Target Language environment during assessment?
    (Average)

    A. Read specific parts of the test as appropriate
    B. Paraphrasing the prompt
    C. Pronouncing vocabulary words
    D. Translating parts of the test

100. Which of the following is an acceptable teaching practice when preparing exceptional students to take tests?
    (Rigorous)

    A. Give practice timed tests
    B. Research topics extensively
    C. Teach additional vocabulary
    D. Write practice essays

101. Which of the following is a possible sign of the gifted ELL student?
 (Average)

 A. Advanced developmental history according to parental interview
 B. Speech delayed in L2
 C. Seems to solve logic problems with difficulty
 D. Good academic performance in L1

102. Which of the following demonstrates test or norming bias?
 (Rigorous)

 A. Administer practice tests with time limits
 B. Negative attitude of the test giver
 C. Translating from L1 to L2 literally
 D. Eliminating ELLs from the school's population

103. If a test question asks a student about an iPod, which kind of bias may the question contain?
 (Rigorous)

 A. Cultural
 B. Attitudinal
 C. Test/Norming
 D. Translation

104. When ELLs are asked to listen to an airport announcement of flight arrivals and departures, which type of test are they being given?
 (Rigorous)

 A. First generation
 B. Second generation
 C. Third generation
 D. Traditional

105. Differentiated instruction is characterized by:
 (Easy)

 A. Different learning goals
 B. The students are placed in learning levels
 C. The gifted student is set a list of learning objectives
 D. Materials are grouped according to ability levels

106. Which one of the following is not true of culture and cultural differences?
 (Average)

 A. Can adversely affect second language learning
 B. Can have a positive effect on second language learning
 C. Determines the outcome of second language learning
 D. May have strong emotional influence on the ELL learner

ESOL PRACTICE TEST

107. Which one of the following is *not* an acceptable practice when working with ELLs?
(Rigorous)

    A. Short wait time
    B. Establishment of group work
    C. Show and tell based on different cultures
    D. Extensive reading time

108. When Mr. Smith planned his class on plants, he brought in plants. He also provided the students with seeds, cotton, and small jars for growing the seeds. Mr. Smith is planning a lesson that is geared towards which type of learner?
(Rigorous)

    A. Tactile
    B. Auditory
    C. Kinesthetic
    D. Visual

109. Which of the following suggestions would *not* create a warm, culturally aware environment?
(Rigorous)

    A. The use of English only in the classroom
    B. Inviting parents to share their experiences with the class
    C. Using scaffolding judiciously
    D. Diversifying the literature/stories in the classroom

110. Which of the following social factors is the single most influential element in second-language learning?
(Average)

    A. Age
    B. Gender
    C. Social conditions
    D. Motivation

111. In Title IX, the Supreme Court ruled that:
(Rigorous)

    A. School districts may not continue education programs that fail to produce positive results for ELLs
    B. Sexual harassment was prohibited in any school activity on or off campus
    C. Students were denied an "equal" education
    D. Discrimination is prohibited against students and employers based on race, ethnicity, national origins, disability, or marital status

112. Which of the following is most appropriate when establishing quality programs for ELLs?
(Rigorous)

    A. Challenge students cognitively
    B. Establishing goals to accommodate all ELLs
    C. Students are encouraged to use their native language
    D. Students need to work independently on L2 goals

113. The American Recovery and Reinvestment Act (2009) established:
    (Rigorous)

    A. Title I
    B. No Child Left Behind Act (NCLB)
    C. That all students must be proficient in math and reading by 2014
    D. Race to the Top (RTT)

114. The No Child Left Behind Act requires schools to:
    (Rigorous)

    A. Include LEPs in some academic assessments
    B. Evaluate LEPs in their native language when possible
    C. Measure LEPs in math and reading once a year in grades 9-12
    D. Show adequate yearly progress

115. Which of the following is *not* a factor of the affective domain that affects language learning?
    (Average)

    A. Age
    B. Anxiety
    C. Teacher expectations
    D. Scaffolding

116. Which one of the following is *not* an affective domain component?
    (Rigorous)

    A. Teacher's expectations
    B. Classroom culture
    C. Language transfer
    D. Motivation

117. Which of the following activities would contribute to an effective classroom culture for ELLs?
    (Rigorous)

    A. Choosing the way in which to present a book report
    B. Working individually on a project
    C. Ambiguous behavioral standards
    D. Fear of classmate's ridicule

118. Which of the following activities would make transitioning from high school to the workplace easier for students?
    (Rigorous)

    A. Visiting the new campus
    B. Holding a Q-and-A session for parents
    C. Visiting with the freshman principal or dean
    D. Talking with former students in a Q-and-A session

119. Which of the following offices would welcome parents who wish to get involved in their children's education?
    (Average)

    A. Youth and family services
    B. TESOL
    C. AAC
    D. NABE

120. Which of the following sources would be the most appropriate to recommend to ELLs for supplementary practice?
    (Rigorous)

    A. http://www2.ed.gov/about/offices/list/ies/index.html?src=oc
    B. http://www.ed.gov/offices/OCR
    C. http://www.eslcafe.com
    D. http://www.ed.gov

ANSWER KEY

1. A	43. D	85. A
2. A	44. A	86. D
3. A	45. D	87. A
4. A	46. B	88. B
5. C	47. C	89. D
6. A	48. B	90. A
7. B	49. C	91. D
8. D	50. A	92. D
9. C	51. D	93. A
10. B	52. D	94. C
11. B	53. C	95. D
12. A	54. C	96. D
13. A	55. C	97. A
14. B	56. D	98. D
15. A	57. D	99. A
16. D	58. D	100. A
17. D	59. D	101. A
18. B	60. B	102. D
19. C	61. D	103. A
20. D	62. A	104. C
21. D	63. C	105. A
22. A	64. A	106. C
23. D	65. C	107. A
24. B	66. C	108. A
25. A	67. C	109. A
26. A	68. C	110. D
27. C	69. C	111. B
28. B	70. D	112. A
29. D	71. A	113. D
30. D	72. C	114. D
31. C	73. B	115. B
32. C	74. B	116. C
33. C	75. D	117. A
34. D	76. D	118. D
35. A	77. D	119. C
36. D	78. B	120. C
37. D	79. C	
38. B	80. B	
39. D	81. C	
40. D	82. D	
41. D	83. D	
42. D	84. C	

Rigor Table

Easy
2, 3, 9, 10, 28, 29, 30, 32, 34, 37, 38, 39, 40, 41, 42, 43, 55, 56, 57, 63, 71, 91, 105

Average
1, 4, 7, 8, 14, 15, 18, 19, 21, 22, 23, 24, 26, 27, 31, 33, 35, 36, 44, 46, 47, 48, 49, 50, 53, 59, 61, 62, 65, 68, 69, 70, 73, 74, 76, 78, 79, 80, 81, 82, 83, 84, 90, 98, 99, 101, 106, 110, 115, 119

Rigorous
5, 6, 11, 12, 13, 16, 17, 20, 25, 45, 51, 52, 54, 58, 60, 64, 66, 67, 72, 75, 77, 85, 86, 87, 88, 89, 92, 93, 94, 95, 96, 97, 100, 102, 103, 104, 107, 108, 109, 111, 112, 113, 114, 116, 117, 118, 120

MTEL ENGLISH AS A SECOND LANGUAGE (ESL) 54 PRACTICE TEST 1 WITH RATIONALES

LISTENING SECTION: ORAL GRAMMAR AND VOCABULARY

Directions: In this part of the actual test, you will hear and read a series of short speeches of nonnative speakers of English. Then you will be asked questions about each student's problems in grammar or vocabulary in the recorded speech. You will be allotted ample time to answer the questions.

1. Listen to an ESOL student talk about his experience with working in the United States.
   (Average)

   (Taped excerpt)

   I'm studying Business Administration. I was in the second semester.

   The verb *was* in the second sentence is incorrect with respect to:

   A. Tense
   B. Gender
   C. Person
   D. Number

Answer: A. Tense
The pronoun *I* is not gender specific, so it may be used for both male and female people. The use of *was* for first person singular is correct in both person and number. However, when discussing current situations, the present tense *am* is the correct tense. Thus, A is the correct option.

ESOL PRACTICE TEST

...en to an ESOL student talking about her mother's food.
(Easy)

(Taped excerpt)

My mom's cooking is too good.

The adverb *too* is incorrect with regards to:

A. Usage
B. Form
C. Spelling
D. Word order

Answer: A. Usage
The form, spelling, and word order are all correct. Therefore, option A must be the incorrect form. The correct usage, in this case, would be the adverb *very*.

3. **Listen to an ESOL student talking about a math grade he received.**
(Easy)

(Taped excerpt)

Just look at this math grade from my teacher. He says I was missing an explanation of my answer.

The verb *was missing* is incorrect with regard to:

A. Tense
B. Agreement
C. Subjunctive
D. Number

Answer: A. Tense
In this case, *was missing* is correct with regards to agreement and number. The subjunctive is not indicated. So, the correct answer is A. The simple past, *missed* is used for reported speech when the speaker is reporting an event in the present.

4. **Listen to an ESOL student talking about her pet bird.**
   (Average)

   (Taped excerpt)

   This bird causes much problems every day.

   The word *much* is incorrect with regard to the use of _____ nouns.

   A. count/no count
   B. regular/irregular
   C. collective
   D. compound

Answer: A. count/no count
Regular/irregular adjectives such as *good/the best* are irrelevant to the word *much*. *Much* is an adjective, not a collective or compound noun. *Much* is used with uncountable nouns. Therefore, A, count/no count nouns is the correct option. *Many*, which is used with plural, countable nouns, would be the correct word.

5. **Listen to an ESOL student talking about having children.**
   (Rigorous)

   (Taped excerpt)

   Many people are afraid of having and to raise children.

   The words *to raise* are incorrect with regard to:

   A. Tense
   B. Agreement
   C. Parallel structure
   D. Adverbial format

Answer: C. Parallel structure
Gerunds have neither tense nor agreement elements. A gerund is a verb form used as a noun, not an adverb. Thus, option C is the correct one. Since the sentence contains both a gerund and an infinitive, one should be changed so both elements have the same structure. The question is phrased so that *to raise* should be changed to *raising*.

6. **Listen to an ESOL student talking to her friend about her beliefs on conducting relationships with others.**
   (Rigorous)

   (Taped excerpt)

   How one behaves towards others is more important than anything else.

   One **refers to:**

   A. You
   B. They
   C. The listener
   D. The speaker

Answer: A. You
In this question, *one* refers to a general *you*. American English generally uses *you* instead of *one*; both, however, are correct. The correct option is A.

7. **Listen to an ESOL student talking about Faulkner's novels.**
   (Average)

   (Taped excerpt)

   Faulkner's books are interesting novels. They are difficult to understand, but it illustrate life in the South.

   The word *it* **is incorrect with respect to:**

   A. Reference
   B. Number
   C. Gender
   D. Class

Answer: B. Number
Gender and class refer to the type of pronoun chosen to be used in oral speech or a written text. *Novels* is the *referent*. The word *it* is a pronoun that should refer back to its antecedent, *novels*. The antecedent *novels* is a countable, plural noun indicating that any pronoun referring back to it should also be plural. Answer B is the correct option for the statement since *it* does not agree in number with its antecedent. The correct pronoun would be *they*.

8. **Listen to an ESOL student talking to her friend about life in the United States.**
    (Average)

    (Taped excerpt)

    I have no stomach for pork.

    The word *stomach* means:

    A. Enlarged storage cavity, in invertebrates
    B. A digestive organ
    C. The abdomen or belly
    D. Appetite for food

Answer: D. Appetite for food
All answers are different definitions of the word stomach. Answer D is the correct response because in this context, the speaker is referring to the ability to eat a certain food, pork.

9. **Listen to an ESOL student talking about her sister's beliefs on eternal love.**
    (Easy)

    (Taped excerpt)

    My sister talks about love all the time. As far as I can see, she makes no sense. Her arguments have neither rhyme or reason.

    The word *or* in the last sentence is incorrect with regard to:

    A. Parallel structure
    B. Usage
    C. Form
    D. Person

Answer: C. Form
Parallel structure, usage, and person do not apply in this case since *neither/nor* is a correlative conjunction. With the negative *neither*, the correct form is *nor*. *Or* is used with the positive *either*. The correct answer is C.

10. Listen to an ESOL student talking about her father.
    (Easy)

    (Taped excerpt)

    My father's name is Jonathan. He was named for her great grandfather.

    The word *her* is incorrect with regard to:

    A. Agreement
    B. Gender
    C. Person
    D. Number

Answer: B. Gender
The third person singular of the verb *to be* is *was* in the past tense, so the agreement of number and person are correct. An incorrect gender has been used since Jonathan is a male name. Thus, *his* would be the correct possessive pronoun. Option B is the best selection.

LISTENING: PRONOUNCIATION

Directions: In this part of the actual test, you will hear and read a series of short speeches of nonnative speakers of English. Then you will be asked questions about each student's problems in pronunciation in the recorded speech. You will not be asked to evaluate the student's grammar or vocabulary usage. To help you answer the questions, the speech will be played a second time. You will be allotted ample time to answer the questions.

11. Listen to an ESOL student reading aloud the following sentence. *(Rigorous)*

    (Taped excerpt)

    The TV program was live. (Student pronounces *live* as [ɪlv].)

    The error in pronunciation in the word *live* indicates a problem with:

    A. Diphthongs
    B. Primary cardinal vowels
    C. Triphthongs
    D. Allophones

Answer: B. Primary cardinal vowels
Diphthongs refer to a combination of two phonemes that glide together. Triphthongs are vowel sounds in which three vowels are sounded in a sequence, such as *fire* or *flower*. Allophones refer to sounds regional speakers make. Thus, answer B is the best option since the pronunciation of the vowel /i/ is in question.

12. **Listen to an ESOL student reading aloud the following sentence.** *(Rigorous)*

    (Taped excerpt)

    Please bring me a hamburger and some fries. (Student pronounces *and* as [aend].)

    The error in pronunciation in the word *and* indicates a problem with:

    A. Elision
    B. Assimilation
    C. Phonemes
    D. Weakness

Answer: A. Elision
Assimilation refers to a phoneme being spoken differently when it is near another phoneme. This is more common in rapid, casual speech. Weakness in English is defined as reduction, assimilation, and elision. The question refers to a specific type of weakness—elision where two phonemes disappear to create an /n/ in typical speech. The best option is A.

13. **Listen to an ESOL student reading aloud the following sentence.** *(Rigorous)*

    (Taped excerpt)

    I am the chairman of the debate club. (Student pronounces *chairman* as [sheərmən].)

    The error in pronunciation of the word *chairman* indicates problems with:

    A. Affricatives
    B. Plosives
    C. Laterals
    D. Glides

Answer: A. Affricatives
English has six plosive consonants. The only consonant classified as a lateral alveolar in English is the /l/. Glides refer to diphthongs where sound does not remain consonant but glides from one sound to another. Affricatives are stop consonants that are released slowly into a period of fricative noise such as the /ch/ in chair. The correct option is A.

14. **Listen to an ESOL student reading aloud the following sentence.** *(Average)*

    (Taped excerpt)

    I believe that my class is starting. (Student pronounces m*y* as [mi].

    The error in pronunciation of the word *my* indicates problems with:

    A. Short vowels
    B. Diphthongs
    C. Triphthongs
    D. Long vowels

Answer: B. Diphthongs
Short vowels are those in such words as *pat, pet, pit, pot,* and *put*. Long vowels are those such as *take, mete, mike, toke,* and *mute*. Triphthongs are vowel sounds in which three vowels are sounded in a sequence, such as *fire* or *flower*. The diphthong [mai] should be used instead of the pure long vowel /i/. Therefore, B is the correct choice.

15. **Listen to an ESOL student reading aloud the following sentence.** *(Average)*

    (Taped excerpt)

    What are you reading? (Student pronounces *are* as [är].)

    The error in pronunciation of the word *are* indicates problems with:

    A. Schwa
    B. Stress
    C. Suprasegmentals
    D. Prosody

Answer: A. Schwa
The speaker does not have problems in stress at the word or sentence level. Suprasegmentals refer to teaching the "big picture," or the characteristics that extend over entire utterances versus teaching individual elements, such as how to pronounce the letter /d/. Stress is an element of prosody; the other is intonation. The schwa /ə/ is used as a symbol to represent an "emptiness" in pronunciation. For example, the /er/ at the end of many words is pronounced using the schwa. The correct answer is A.

16. **Listen to an ESOL student reading aloud the following sentence.** *(Rigorous)*

(Taped excerpt)

I would like a thin slice of cheesecake. (Student pronounces *thin* as [ðin].)

The error in pronunciation of the word *thin* indicates problems with:

A. Labials
B. Affricatives
C. Palatals
D. Fricatives

Answer: D. Fricatives
Labials refer to a group of consonants in which the lips form their distinctive sound. The palatals are those sounds made by raising the front of the tongue towards the hard palate. Affricatives are stop consonants that are released slowly into a period of fricative noise such as the /ch/ in church. The /th/ sound in English is represented as a dental fricative and may be voiced /θ/ or voiceless /ð/. The /th/ sound in thin is voiced and represented by the /θ/.

17. Listen to an ESOL student reading aloud the following sentence. *(Rigorous)*

(Taped excerpt)

I want to be a marine scientist. (Student pronounces *want to be* as [want to be].)

The error in pronunciation of the words *want to be* indicates problems with:

A. Fricatives
B. Assimilation
C. Linking
D. Elision

Answer: D. Elision
Assimilation refers to a phoneme being spoken differently when it is near another phoneme. This is more common in rapid, casual speech. Linking refers to sounds that join with the following sounds to produce a linked sound, such as Alice in Wonderland where the /c/ becomes an /s/ and links with *in* to become /sin/. Weakness in English is defined as reduction, assimilation, and elision. The question refers to a specific type of weakness—elision where three phonemes appear together. The most likely scenario is that native speakers would join the words pronouncing phonemes as [wannabe]. The best option is D.

18. **Listen to an ESOL student reading aloud the following sentence.** *(Average)*

    (Taped excerpt)

    I saw *The King's Speech* last night. (Student pronounces and emphasizes each word.)

    The error in speaking the sentence indicates problems with:

    A. Intonation
    B. Linking sounds
    C. Pitch
    D. Stress-timing

Answer: B. Linking sounds
Intonation concerns the tone pattern of speech and is produced by changing the vocal pitch. Pitch refers to the rising/falling pattern of the voiced speech. Some linguists refer to English as a stress-timed language whereas many other languages, for instance, Spanish, are syllable-timed. If a student pronounces and emphasizes each word, then the student has trouble with linking sounds since *last night* would surely be linked as /lasnight/.

19. **Listen to an ESOL student reading aloud the following sentence.** *(Average)*

    (Taped excerpt)

    The band has just signed with a new record label. (Student pronounces *record* as [re/CORD].)

    The error in pronunciation of the word *record* indicates problems with:

    A. Pitch
    B. Reduction
    C. Stress
    D. Rhythm

Answer: C. Stress
Pitch refers to the high or low tone of the voice. Stress refers to accent. Reduction has to do with the speaker reducing certain phonemes in order to produce simpler, easier-to-pronounce utterances. Rhythm is the sound pattern achieved through stressed and unstressed syllables. The stress, or accent, of certain words in English changes their grammatical function in an utterance. The word [re/CORD] is a transitive verb. The correct word should be [REC/ord], an adjective. C is the best option.

20. **Listen to an ESOL student reading aloud the following sentence.** *(Rigorous)*

    (Taped excerpt)

    What do you plan to do after graduation? (Student pronounces *graduation* with a rising voice.)

    The error in pronunciation of the word *graduation* indicates problems with:

    A. Pitch
    B. Stress
    C. Function words
    D. Intonation

Answer: D. Intonation
Pitch refers to the high or low tone of the voice. Stress refers to accent. Grammatical or function words are words that show how other words and sentences relate to each other, e.g., *in, the, which,* etc. Intonation concerns the pattern of pitch and stress changes uttered in a phrase or a sentence. In English, the intonation of the final word usually drops instead of rising. The best option is D.

FOUNDATIONS OF LINGUISTICS AND LANGUAGE LEARNING

Directions: In this part of the test, you will read a series of short writing samples produced by nonnative speakers of English. You will be asked to identify the errors in the students' writing. Therefore, before taking the test, you should be familiar with the writing of nonnative speakers who are learning English.

Questions 21-23 are based on the following excerpt from an essay describing a popular sport in the student's native country.

> *Soccer of my country is a very popular sport in every city. Soccer players must has skill kicking the ball. They train every day so that he can become superstars.*

21. In the first sentence, the error is in the relative order of: *(Average)*

    A. A noun and an adjective
    B. The direct and indirect objects
    C. The subject and object
    D. The prepositional phrases

Answer: D. The prepositional phrases
The error lies in the order of the first two prepositional phrases. The sentence should read *Soccer is a very popular sport in every city of my country....* Prepositional phrases normally are placed as close to the words they modify as possible to avoid confusion. Answer D is the correct option.

22. The second sentence contains an error in the: *(Average)*

    A. Agreement between the pronoun and verb
    B. Pronoun antecedent and referent
    C. Structure of the subordinate clause
    D. Order of the sentence elements

Answer: A. Agreement between the pronoun and verb
The sentence should read *Soccer players must have...* Therefore the correct option is A.

23. The last sentence contains an error in the:
(Average)

   A. Noun and an adjective
   B. Direct and indirect objects
   C. Subject and the object
   D. Pronoun form

Answer: D. Pronoun form
In the last sentence, the antecedent of *they* is *soccer players*. Therefore, the plural form of the subject (nominative) pronoun should be used in the phrase so that *they* can become superstars. The correct option is D.

Questions 24-26 are based on an excerpt from an essay describing the student's favorite foods.

> *My favorite food for breakfast is a cup of hot chocolate with a bread and a piece of cheese. In my country we eat a lot of beef and beans. There are always any beans for every meal. There is also rice at every meal too. Visitors in my country likes to eat fruit or arequipe for dessert.*

24. In the first sentence, there is an error in the:
(Average)

   A. Verb tense
   B. Parallel structure
   C. Punctuation
   D. Subject and object

Answer: B. Parallel structure
The items in this series (...a bread and a piece of cheese) should all have the same structure. They should all be nouns, gerunds, or prepositional phrases but not mixed together. Thus, Answer B is the correct answer.

25. **In the third sentence, the word *any* is incorrect because:**
    (Rigorous)

    A. *Some* is used with count nouns
    B. *Any* is used with noncount nouns
    C. *Any* is used in questions
    D. *Any* is used in negative statements

Answer: A. *Some* is used with count nouns
Statements B, C, and D are correct statements about the use of *any*. Both *some* and *any* can be used with count nouns, but the meaning is different. *Any* in this sentence would imply that there are some beans, but it would not matter how many or what kind, as in *he can't tolerate any criticism*. In this case, *some* should be used to express the idea of an unspecified quantity. Therefore, A is the correct choice.

26. **In sentence 5, the correct form of the verb *likes* should be:**
    (Average)

    A. like
    B. liked
    C. will like
    D. have liked

Answer: A. like
The author is discussing that visitors enjoy eating fruit or arequipe for desert — always. Therefore, the simple present tense is used. It should agree with the subject *visitors,* and thus must be plural. Selection A is the correct option.

Directions: Each of the questions or statements that follow is followed by four possible answers or completions. Select the one that is best in each of the remaining questions.

ESOL PRACTICE TEST

27. ***Eight*** **and** ***ate*** **are examples of which phonographemic differences?**
    (Average)

    A. Homonyms
    B. Homographs
    C. Homophones
    D. Heteronyms

Answer: C. Homophones
Homonyms is a general term for words with two or more meanings. *Homographs* are two or more words with the same spelling or pronunciation (usually), but have different meanings. Sometimes the pronunciation is different. *Heteronyms* are two or more words that have the same spelling but different meanings and spellings. *Homophones* are words that have the same pronunciation, but different meanings and spellings. C is the correct response.

28. ***Bow (to bend), bow (front part of a ship),*** **and bow (***a decorative knot***) are examples of which phonographemic differences?**
    (Easy)

    A. Homonyms
    B. Homographs
    C. Homophones
    D. Heteronyms

Answer: B. Homographs
See explanation for question 27.

29. **In the statement** *Fido got bitten by a huge snake*, **the stress would fall on which word?**
    (Easy)

    A. Fido
    B. got bitten
    C. huge
    D. snake

Answer: D. snake
In English, the stress falls on the new information being imparted. Most probably the new information is what bit Fido, and thus, *snake* is the important new information. The correct option is D.

30. In *morphemic analysis*, you need to study:
    (Easy)

    A. The smallest unit within a language system to which meaning is attached
    B. The way in which speech sounds form patterns
    C. The way the word is spelled
    D. The root word and the suffix and/or prefix

Answer: D. The root word and the suffix and/or prefix
The study of the way in which speech sounds form patterns is called phonology. The smallest unit within a language system to which meaning is attached is merely the definition of a morpheme. The root word and the suffix and/or prefix are components of morphemes and basic to the analysis of a word. Therefore, the correct answer is D.

31. The study of *morphemes* helps the student understand:
    (Average)

    A. How to sound out a word
    B. Diphthongs
    C. Grammatical information
    D. Predicates

Answer: C. Grammatical information
The sound of a word is its phonology. Diphthongs are complex speech sounds or glides that begin with one vowel and gradually change to another vowel within the same syllable. Predicates are the verbs and one of the eight parts of speech. The correct answer is C. Grammatical morphemes give information to show how the parts of a sentence relate to each other. Grammatical information is useful when determining which parts of the sentence are related to each other.

32. If you are studying *semantics*, then you are studying:
    (Easy)

    A. Intonation and accent when conveying a message
    B. Culture
    C. The definition of individual words and meanings
    D. The subject-verb-object order of the English sentence

Answer: C. The definition of individual words and meanings
The intonation and accent used when conveying a message refer to pitch and stress. Culture includes all of the elements pertaining to a specific society. The subject-verb-object order of the English sentence is an element of syntax, or the grammatical combination of words and phrases. C is the best option. The definition of individual words and meanings is semantics.

33. **Which one of the following is *not* included in the study of syntax?**
    (Average)

    A. The parts of speech
    B. The parts of a sentence
    C. Inflections of different words
    D. Sentence transformations

Answer: C. Inflections of different words
Since syntax is the grammar of a language, option C is the best response. Inflections of different words in English occur only as suffixes and are studied under morphology.

34. **In the following sentence: "I had a few nuts before my meal" which word is an example of a countable, common noun?**
    (Easy)

    A. I
    B. had
    C. few
    D. nuts

Answer: D. nuts
Option A is incorrect since I is a pronoun. Option B is a verb. Option C is used when referring to countable nouns but is an adjective. Option D is the correct choice since nuts may be counted.

35. **To which subcategory of subordinating conjunction does *as soon as* belong?**
    (Average)

    A. Time
    B. Cause and effect
    C. Contrast
    D. Condition

Answer: A. Time
Option B, cause and effect conjunctions, includes *because, now that, since,* etc. Option C, refers to conjunctions such as *although, even though, though,* etc. Condition conjunctions (Option D) include *if, unless, whether or not,* etc. Time conjunctions (Option A) are those referring to time, such as: *after, before, while,* etc. Option A is the correct choice.

36. **Which kind of sentence is the following sentence: "When the tornado was near, the sky darkened and the wind grew stronger."**
    (Average)

    A. Simple sentence
    B. Compound sentence
    C. Complex sentence
    D. Compound-complex sentence

Answer: D. Compound-complex sentence
The sentence includes two independent clauses: *The sky darkened and the wind grew stronger (compound) and* one dependent clause: *when the tornado was near* (complex). Thus our sentence becomes compound-complex.

37. **To change the active voice sentence "The poet read the poem" to a passive voice sentence, the correct form would be:**
    (Easy)

    A. The poem read the poet.
    B. The poem is being read by the poet.
    C. The poem is read by the poet.
    D. The poem was read by the poet.

Answer: D. The poem was read by the poet.
The correct form of the past tense "read" would be "was read". Thus, the correct answer is D.

38. **When a teacher says: "Please sit down" she is trying to get the students to do something. This is an example of:**
    (Easy)

    A. Synonyms
    B. Speech acts
    C. Culture in the classroom
    D. Body language

Answer: B. Speech acts
Option A: Synonyms refers to two words that mean the same. The statement "Please sit down" has no particular cultural significance and the teacher is not using body language when she makes a simple statement. The best option is B, where the speaker is engaged in a speech act or an utterance designed to get people to do something.

39. When someone warns "Don't miss the boat", the speaker is using a/an: *(Easy)*

- A. Cognate
- B. Derivational morpheme
- C. Phrase
- D. Idiom

Answer: D. Idiom
Idioms are new meanings assigned to words that already have a meaning in a language. The expression *Don't miss the boat* literally means a watercraft is about to depart. However, it has become an idiomatic way to say that you should *not delay doing something so long as to lose an opportunity.*

40. The French word "bleu" and the English word "blue" are examples of: *(Easy)*

- A. Heteronyms
- B. Transformations
- C. Idioms
- D. Cognates

Answer: D. Cognates
Heteronyms are words which have the same spelling but a different pronunciation and spelling (in the same language). Transformations refer to the ability to add, delete, or permute informational content. Idioms are words or phrases used in new and different ways from their original meaning. Cognates are words which are similar in different languages, and one may assume to have the same meaning. Some of these are not true cognates and are known as false cognates. An example would be the English words "library" and the Spanish word "librería". The correct option is D because both words refer to a color.

41. **What has been the most important factor in the growth of English?**
 (Easy)

    A. The invasion of the Germanic tribes in England
    B. The pronunciation changes in Middle English
    C. The extension of the British Empire
    D. The introduction of new words from different cultures

Answer: D. The introduction of new words from different cultures
The sun never set on the British Empire during the 19th century causing English to spread all over the world. Options A and B have had little effect on the growth of modern English. Many cultures, such as France and Spain, try to restrict the introduction of foreign words into their languages. However, English has grown constantly through the introduction of new words from different cultures around the world. Too, modern technology has introduced numerous new words into English. Thus, Option D is the correct one.

42. **When people in the same profession use language to communicate, they frequently use _____ to communicate their thoughts.**
 (Easy)

    A. code switching
    B. cognates
    C. elaborated code
    D. jargon

Answer: D. jargon
Code switching involves moving between two or more language with ease, such as between bilingual speakers. Cognates are words of similar origins in different languages. Elaborated code is used when the speakers are not of the same background. Jargon is specialized, work-related language used to avoid lengthy explanations between members of the same profession, such as ESOL professionals who distinguish between ESL, EFL, TESOL, and ELL. Option D is the correct answer.

43. If you are studying *disglossia*, then you are studying:
(Easy)

- A. The definition of individual words and meanings
- B. How context impacts the interpretation of language
- C. Meaning that is stored or inherent, as well as contextual
- D. The use of separate dialects to the use of separate languages

Answer: D. The use of separate dialects to the use of separate languages
The definition of individual words and meanings refers to semantics. Meaning which is stored or inherent, as well as contextual refers to the lexicon of a language. There is no special term used to identify how context impacts on the interpretation of language. The best option is D since *disglossia* ranges from the study of the use of separate dialects to the use of separate languages in language communities.

44. Register refers to the language used depending on:
(Average)

- A. The relationship between the speakers
- B. The communicative competence of the speakers
- C. The polite discourse involved
- D. The culture of the speakers

Answer: A. The relationship between the speakers
The communicative competence of the speakers certainly affects their register, but communicative competence is the ability to use language correctly and appropriately in different situations. Polite discourse is the use of "empty speech" or perfunctory speech that has little meaning but is important in social exchanges, such as "How are you?" The culture of the speakers influences how speakers address each other. Some cultures do not look you straight in the eye as English speakers do. People change their register depending on the relationship between the speakers, the formality of the situation, and the attitudes towards the listeners and the subject. Answer A is the correct option.

45. In analyzing World Englishes, Kachru classified countries as members of:
(Rigorous)

   A. Former colonies and colonialists
   B. First world and third world countries
   C. Dominate cultures and subordinate cultures
   D. Inner, outer, and expanding circles

Answer: D. Inner, outer, and expanding circles
The outer circle is made up of ex-colonies of the traditional English speaking countries. In the inner circle are the traditional English-speaking countries such as the United Kingdom, the United States, Ireland, New Zealand, Australia, and Canada. The expanding circle contains countries that are learning English for reasons of information technology, travel, work, and business. D is the correct answer.

46. English as it is spoken around the world is referred to as _____.
(Average)

   A. the Queen's English
   B. world English
   C. substandard English
   D. Standard American English

Answer: B. world English
Options A and D refer to the standard speech of the UK and the USA respectively. Option C is not correct since many non-native speakers around the world speak fluent, grammatically correct English as a result of years of formalized study. Option B is a term that has constantly grown in popularity since the 1960s referring to English in all its varieties. Speakers of World English are believed to outnumber native English speakers. Option B is the best choice.

47. Skinner's "operant conditioning" was based upon his belief that language was learned by:
(Average)

   A. Interaction with their environment
   B. New knowledge must be reconciled with old
   C. Stimulus-response actions
   D. A language acquisition device

Answer: C. Stimulus-response actions
The functional, developmental, or interactionist theories of language learning include both Options A: interaction with their environment and B: new knowledge must be reconciled with old knowledge. Option D: a language acquisition device was theorized by Chomsky to explain the ability of children to learn a language regardless of which language. The correct choice is C where a prompt is given and the learner responds.

48. In Gattegno's *Silent Way*, students:
(Average)

   A. Repeat the phrases spoken by the teacher
   B. Carefully study charts, gestures, and hints from the teacher
   C. The students must remain silent
   D. The instructor uses abundance speech to teach the sound system

Answer: B. Carefully study, charts, gestures, and hints from the teacher
The essence of the Silent Way is that the teacher remains silent and the students speak. In the first class, the teacher explains the theory, and thereafter, remains silent while the students try to create language. Option B is the correct choice.

49. **A teacher who instructs students to "Open the door" or "Go to the whiteboard" is using which basic language approach/method?** *(Average)*

    A. The Silent Way
    B. Notional/functional
    C. Total Physical Response (TPR)
    D. Natural Approach

Answer: C. Total Physical Response (TPR)
A teacher using Option A, the Silent Way, would not instruct students in dialogs but expect them to construct their own. Option B the notional/functional approach was based on the idea of notions (location, frequency, time, etc.) and functions (requests, threats, complaints, etc.) that students needed to know in order to communicate. The notional (sequence of events) and functional (buying a computer) would provide adult learners with the concepts they would use in their daily lives. Option D, the Natural Approach, emphasizes "natural speech," so pre-written dialogs would violate this principle. Option C, TPR, uses physical movements to follow basic instructions. Option C is the best choice.

50. **By learning lexical chunks, English language learners (ELLs) develop:** *(Average)*

    A. Lexis
    B. Fluency
    C. Jargon
    D. Private speech

Answer: A. Lexis
Option B may be excluded since fluency is not necessarily improved by learning only lexical chunks. Jargon is relatively unimportant except to speakers of the same group. It is usually work-related. Option D refers to a pre-speaking phase of L2 development. Option C, lexical chunks, proposed by Lewis suggests that LLs who learn fixed and semi-fixed chunks (blocks) of language that do not change increases their lexis (vocabulary) considerably. C is the best choice.

51. Prabhu was most closely associated with which methodology?
(Rigorous)

- A. Subordinate teaching to learning
- B. Notional/functional syllabus
- C. Delayed oral response
- D. Reasoning and problem solving

Answer: D. Reasoning and problem solving
Option A: Gattegno was associated with the Silent Way whose cardinal principle was "subordinate teaching to learning". Option B: Wilkins developed the Notional/Functional Syllabus based on meanings a learner needed to communicate. Option C: delayed oral response was developed by the Russian Postovsky. The correct option is D. Prabhu who developed the idea of "gap" activities, which include reasoning and problem solving.

52. A second-language learner who is in the formulaic speech level is in which stage of development?
(Rigorous)

- A. Knows 500 receptive words
- B. Knows 1000 receptive words
- C. Knows 3000 receptive words
- D. Knows 6000 receptive words

Answer: D. Knows 6000 receptive words
The options show the silent period, private speech, lexical chunk, and formulaic speech levels in order of development. The final stage is experimental or simplified speech when the learner has developed a level of fluency and can make semantic and grammatical generalizations. Option D is the correct choice.

53. Syntax is acquired by second-language learners:
(Average)

- A. At the same rate in L1 and L2
- B. Faster in L2 than L1
- C. In the same order as L1
- D. In different order than L1

Answer: C. In the same order as L1
All language learners must progress through the same hierarchical steps in their language learning process. They go from the least to the most complicated stages regardless of whether it is in the L1 or L2.

54. Code-switching refers to the ability of the speaker to:
(Rigorous)

   A. Use dialect appropriately
   B. Develop an inter-language
   C. Switch languages to express oneself
   D. Use empty speech

Answer: C. Switch languages to express oneself
A dialect is any form or variety of a spoken language peculiar to a region, community, social group, etc. Interlanguage is the language spoken by ELLs that is between their L1 and L2. Empty or formulaic speech refers to speech that is ritualistic in nature and perhaps used for social politeness rather than information. It is also called empty language. People may switch languages (code) when a word is not known in the language being spoken at the moment. Option C is the correct option.

55. Which of the following is a strategy of language-learners?
(Easy)

   A. Communicative competence
   B. Bilingualism
   C. Interlanguage
   D. Interference

Answer: C. Interlanguage
Communicative competence and bilingualism are goals of language learners. Interlanguage occurs when the second language learner lacks proficiency in L2 and tries to compensate for his or her lack of fluency in the new language. Three components are overgeneralization, simplification, and L1 interference or language transfer. Therefore, C is the correct answer.

56. **The inability of a language student to conjugate verb forms is probably an example of:**
(Easy)

- A. Private speech
- B. Cognitive factors that affect speech
- C. Interference
- D. Fossilization

Answer: D. Fossilization
Private speech is a stage of second-language development. Cognitive factors such as age, intelligence, cognitive style, and personality will affect language development, but the question refers to one specific type of language learning problem. Interference occurs when a rule from L1 interferes negatively with the development of L2 language. Fossilization happens when a language learner reaches a plateau in the development of the new language and cannot achieve full fluency because of a specific developmental problem which varies with individual learners. The correct answer is D.

57. **Which of the following is an example of a language learner having problems with simplification?**
(Easy)

- A. Occurs when the learner adds -ed to all verbs
- B. Might say "I like sky the blue."
- C. Hispanics pronouncing words like *student* as *estudent*
- D. Asking someone if "You like?" instead of "Do you like this one?"

Answer: D. Asking someone if "You like?" instead of "Do you like this one?"
Overgeneralization means applying the same rule to all examples, such as in Option A. Option B and C are examples of interference. Simplification is a common learner error involving simplifying the language where the correct structures have not been internalized. In this case, the correct question form has not been acquired though the ELL's meaning is clear, such as in Option D.

ESOL PRACTICE TEST

58. According to Krashen, English language learners acquire which of the following language structures last?
    (Rigorous)

    A. Auxiliary verb, article
    B. Irregular past tense verbs
    C. –ing, copula
    D. Possessives

Answer: D. Possessives
The correct order of acquisition is Option C, B, A, and D. The regular past tense verbs, 3rd person singular, and possessives are acquired in the last stage of acquisition. D is the correct answer.

59. Which of the following is an example of intrinsic motivation in relation to language learning?
    (Average)

    A. A need based on job requirements
    B. A parental imposition on a child
    C. A need caused by living in a bilingual community
    D. A desire to know another culture more intimately

Answer: D. A desire to know another culture more intimately
Options A, B, and C are all examples of extrinsic motivation—motivation imposed by external needs. Option D is a personal wish or desire that comes from within a person, and therefore, the correct choice.

60. What type of scaffolding is the teacher demonstrating when she places students together in work groups?
    (Rigorous)

    A. Interactive
    B. Shared
    C. Modeling
    D. Independent

Answer: B. Shared
In Options A and C, the teacher plays a key role in the scaffolding. Option D is reached when the language learner no longer needs help to achieve academic success. Option B: Shared occurs as students work together pooling their knowledge (and that of the teacher if necessary) to solve problems or complete projects. The best choice is B.

61. Which one of the following is an effective question in a guided scaffolding activity?
(Average)

    A. Can you tell me the purpose of this activity?
    B. What is the name of this plant?
    C. Which one of you started the clock?
    D. Do you remember last week when we classified other plants?

Answer: D. Do you remember last week when we classified other plants?
Options A, B, and C are asking for specific details and are lower order questions. Only Option D is giving students a clue and reminding them of previous knowledge. It is the correct option as it guides students in the right direction to complete the task.

62. According to Krashen and Terrell's *Acquisition Hypothesis*, language learning is:
(Average)

    A. Subconscious learning and conscious learning
    B. Formal study
    C. An invariable path
    D. Comprehensible input

Answer: A. Subconscious learning and conscious learning
Krashen and Terrell's Acquisition Hypothesis states that language learning occurs when the subconscious processes natural communication where the emphasis is on communication (acquisition) and "learning" which occurs during formal study of the properties of language. A is the correct choice.

63. The researcher most closely associated with communicative competence is:
(Easy)

    A. Bernstein
    B. Fishman
    C. Hymes
    D. Labov

Answer: C. Hymes
Bernstein was closely associated with the restricted and elaborated codes. Fishman furthered the studies of Ferguson on disglossia. Labov's work concentrated on dialects, specifically the African American Vernacular. Hymes' work focused on communicative competence and is the correct choice.

64. **Though there are exceptions, the most common purposes of a narrative are to:**
    (Rigorous)

    A. Tell a story or incident, explain a process, or explain cause and effect
    B. Inform people or persuade them to act or think differently about a topic
    C. Used to stimulate the senses which support the text or create spatial in a text
    D. Divide, define, or compare and contrast

Answer: A. Tell a story or incident, explain a process, or explain cause and effect
Option B is the purpose of evaluative text. Option C states the purposes of a descriptive text. Option D defines the purposes of classification texts. Option A states the purposes of descriptive texts and is the correct choice.

65. **In a top-down strategy of literacy development, which one of the following undesirable strategies might a reader use?**
    (Average)

    A. Read words
    B. Read phrases
    C. Ignore title and typeface
    D. Achieves general understanding

Answer: C. Ignore title and typeface
Options A, B, and D are all steps in a bottom-up strategy. Only Option C is an undesirable reading strategy in the top-down model. Both the title and typeface contain clues to total understanding of a reading passage. Option C is undesirable and the correct answer.

66. **According to Ehri's continuum of word reading development, which one of the following belongs to the mature alphabetic phase of the alphabetic principle?**
    (Rigorous)

    A. Tries to remember words by incidental visual characteristics
    B. Relies on letter names to identify words
    C. Can represent almost every sound with a logical letter choice
    D. Remembers multisyllabic words

Answer: C. Can represent almost every sound with a logical letter choice
According to Ehri's continuum, Option A is the logographic phase, Option B is the novice alphabetic phase, Option C is the mature alphabetic phase, and Option D is the orthographic phase. D is the correct choice.

67. According to Collier, parents should *not* use a second language in the home because:
(Rigorous)

   A. They will make many mistakes
   B. They may experience difficulties in expressing themselves
   C. They are working below their actual cognitive level
   D. Their children receive sufficient L2 instruction in their schools

Answer: C. They are working below their actual cognitive level
Collier believes that it was a disservice to insist that parents not use their native language because they would be working at a level below their cognitive maturity. He believed that parents should feel free to use their native language in speaking with their children. Option C is the correct choice.

68. Which of the following options is considered to be a reason for continuing to develop L1 literacy with English Language Learners (ELLs)?
(Average)

   A. L2 literacy is achieved quicker
   B. Subtle L2 pragmatics can be understood better
   C. More mature cognitive development is achieved
   D. Learning L2 vocabulary is easier

Answer: C. More mature cognitive development is achieved
Options A, B, and D may be possible but are not necessarily so. Native speakers bring many positive features from their first language skills that can be transferred to L2 learning. However, given the complexities and numerous languages in the world, such blanket statements are hard to prove with research. Only Option C is an advantage to continuing L1that has been thoroughly researched by Collier. The correct answer is C.

69. The direct method involves:
(Average)

   A. Commands that students must carry out
   B. The use of vivid pictures and choices
   C. Use of oral language and grammar learned inductively
   D. A story is dictated to be practice read

Answer: C. Use of oral language and grammar learned inductively
Total Physical Response involves carrying out commands. The Natural Approach uses vivid pictures and choices to introduce new vocabulary and experiences. The Whole Language Approach teaches children language through the use of a story they dictate and practice reading. The Direct Method uses oral language and grammar learned inductively to build up oral communication skills. Option C is the correct choice.

70. **Which of the following is *not* a benefit of storytelling according to Wajnryb?**
    (Average)

    A. It appeals to the affective domain
    B. It reduces anxiety by forging listening experience
    C. It is pedagogically positive
    D. It is artificial communication

Answer: D. It is artificial communication
According to Wajnryb, A, B, and C are all positive benefits of storytelling. Answer D is incorrect because Wajnryb considers storytelling to be genuine communication. Therefore, D is the correct choice.

71. **Which of the following models' goal is bilingualism?**
    (Easy)

    A. Indigenous language immersion
    B. Pull-out ESL
    C. SDAIE
    D. Transition

Answer: A. Indigenous language immersion
The most commonly used model is the pull-out ESL whose goal is English proficiency. SDAIE or Specially Designed Academic Programs in English is the structured immersion model most commonly used in California. The goal is English language proficiency. Transition models provided approximately three years of BICS but frequently leave the LEP with almost no support while learning CALP. Only the Indigenous language immersion model is socially, linguistically, and cognitively attuned to the native culture and community, Option A is the correct choice.

72. **In student-centered learning the teacher's role is that of a _____?**
    (Rigorous)

    A. guide
    B. cheerleader
    C. facilitator
    D. coach

Answer: C. facilitator
Teachers are frequently asked to take on all the roles mentioned. However, in student-centered learning, students must assume active roles and the responsibility for their own learning. The teacher is a facilitator. Option C is the best choice.

73. **In teaching English Language Learners, which of the following is a valid reason for using peer tutoring?**
    (Average)

    A. To relieve tension
    B. To reinforce learning in the tutor
    C. To allow students to learn in a different mode
    D. To practice English at will

Answer: B. To reinforce learning in the tutor
Option D refers to educational technologies where the machines never become tired and students can use them at will. While Options A and C could be valid reasons for changing classroom instruction by using another method, they are not the primary reasons for peer tutoring. At the same time as the tutored student gains more insight, the tutor reinforces his/her learning. Therefore, Option B is the correct answer.

74. **Which of the following reasons is an advantage to using machines in the ESOL classroom?**
    (Average)

    A. They are inexpensive
    B. They are nonjudgmental
    C. They are fun
    D. They are better than teachers

Answer: B. They are nonjudgmental
Options A and D are highly doubtful. Option C is questionable. Many educational technology programs are fun; using the equipment itself can be challenging. Only Option B is a valid reason for using educational technologies in the language classroom. B is the correct choice.

75. **Which one of the following teaching practices is *not* a valid listening comprehension strategy?**
    (Rigorous)

    A. Listening for discourse markers
    B. Use of good reading texts
    C. Using repetition and facial expressions
    D. Summarizing and retelling stories

Answer: D. Summarizing and retelling stories
Options A, B, and C are all valid listening strategies. Option D, the summarizing and retelling of stories is a speaking strategy. Answer D is the correct choice.

76. **Why would the average Spanish speaking ELL need extra work on the English vowels?**
    (Average)

    A. English vowels are different from L1 of the Spanish speaker
    B. There is no sound-symbol correspondence in the English vowels
    C. Spelling of English vowels and their sounds is easy
    D. English has multiple vowel sounds

Answer: D. English has multiple vowel sounds
Option A may be eliminated because the vowels are the same in both languages. There is some sound-symbol correspondence in English, but not always, so Option B would be a doubtful choice. Option C, the spelling of English vowels and their sounds is easy, is incorrect as the spelling of English vowel and their sounds can be difficult since the same sound can be spelled various ways. Option D is the best choice as there are multiple vowel sounds represented by the English vowels and consonants.

77. **Which one of the following is *not* a strategy used in content-based learning?**
    (Rigorous)

    A. Accessing prior knowledge
    B. Modifying state-mandated, content-area textbooks
    C. Providing comprehensible feedback
    D. Allowing 10 minutes free-reading time after recess

Answer: D. Allowing 10 minutes free-reading time after recess
The key to content-based learning is incorporating content-related learning into activities while instructing the needed language skills at the same time, as in Options A, B, and C. The best choice is D, which is designed as a classroom management technique and the relationship between the content and its instructional strategy is minimal.

78. **Which one of the following is *not* a metacognitive learning strategy?**
    (Average)

    A. Review a key concept
    B. Skim for information
    C. Create optimal learning conditions
    D. Keeping track of errors

Answer: B. Skim for information
Options A, C, and D are all metacognitive learning strategies. Answer B is a cognitive strategy and the correct choice.

79. **Which researcher(s) is(are) most closely associated with the schema theory?**
    (Average)

    A. Rossell & Baker
    B. Gersten
    C. Carrell & Eisterhold
    D. Lambert

Answer: C. Carrell & Eisterhold
Rossell & Baker (1996) concluded that there is little evidence that bilingual education works. Gersten (2000, 2001) proposed early exit from English language support programs, more assistance for special needs students including ELLs, and reduced English language demands when students are challenged cognitively. Lambert is a proponent of the Transitional Bilingual Education Model. The schema theory of Carrell & Eisterhold suggests that schemata must be related to previous knowledge or learning does not take place. When activated, schemata are able to evaluate the new materials in light of previous knowledge. Option C is the correct choice.

80. **Incorporating prior knowledge into L2 learning permits ELLs to:**
    (Average)

    A. Permits readers to learn and remember less
    B. Improves reading comprehension
    C. Avoids in-depth study
    D. Stimulates a lack of comprehension

Answer: B. Improves reading comprehension
Activating schemata and incorporating previous knowledge into L2 learning will strengthen the learning process. It certainly does not cause readers to learn and remember less, avoid in-depth study, or stimulates a lack of comprehension. Option B is the correct choice.

81. **Which of the following instructional strategies would promote fluency?**
    (Average)

    A. Playing vocabulary games
    B. Explicit study of vocabulary lists
    C. Role plays
    D. Using computer language games

Answer: C. Role plays
Answers A, B, and D may be discarded as options since the learning vocabulary in isolated contexts will increase knowledge but not necessarily improve fluency. Only Answer C suggests a way in which fluency is developed by speaking practice in a nonthreatening way.

82. According to many, the easiest single strategy for remembering new vocabulary is:
    (Average)

    A. Names placed on classroom objects
    B. Learning new words from special lists
    C. TPR activities
    D. Singing

Answer: D. Singing
Answers A, B, and C are all valuable ways to learn new vocabulary. However, many report that D. Singing is the easiest way to remember new vocabulary.

83. Which of the following reasons is a valid reason for providing different material on the same subject to a classroom of ELL students?
    (Average)

    A. It's easier than summarizing all the material
    B. Different textbooks cover different aspects of the subject
    C. Students need to fill in their Know-Want-Learn charts by reading a lot
    D. No two people learn alike

Answer: D. No two people learn alike
Conscientious teachers would reject Option A. Option B is valid if the teacher needs to cover different aspects of the subject for high performing students. However, most teachers will try to focus on specific aspects and not provide additional materials that might confuse ELLs or low ability students. Option C is a valid teaching strategy, but it possibly causes unnecessary levels of difficulty for the task. The best option is D.

84. Realia often is used in classrooms. Which one of the following would be a valid example of realia for teaching about genetics?
    (Average)

    A. A set of different colored gemstones
    B. A balance scale
    C. Gerbils of different colors
    D. A pizza

Answer: C. Gerbils of different colors
A, C, and D are examples of realia which could be used for different purposes. However, gerbils of different colors and sizes would be a sure-fire way to capture the interest of students. Answer D is the best choice.

ESOL PRACTICE TEST

85. **One reason young children are often considered better language learners than older children or an adult is children:**
    (Rigorous)

    A. Are more emotionally open to learning a new language
    B. Have more access to comprehensible input
    C. Are able to use inductive reasoning
    D. Are tied to their native language and culture

Answer: A. Are more emotionally open to learning a new language
Answer B is dubious since teens and adults have considerably more freedom than children. Answer C is true of teens and older learners, but in children inductive reasoning is not fully developed. Answer D also refers to the attachment to their native culture of teens and older learners. The correct answer is A. Younger learners are more receptive to working through the problems of a new language without restrictions that come with age and the need to save face, be in control, etc. A is the best choice.

86. **Which of the learning tendencies (Reid, 1987) most accurately describes a student who enjoys doing lab experiments?**
    (Rigorous)

    A. Visual
    B. Auditory
    C. Kinesthetic
    D. Tactile

Answer: D. Tactile
A visual learner learns from seeing words on the board or reading. An auditory learner learns from hearing words spoken, from oral explanations, and from listening to tapes or lectures. A kinesthetic learner learns by experience or by being physically involved. The best choice is D where the learner is enjoys hands-on learning, learning by doing, working on models and lab experiments among others.

87. **Which of the following is the most common method for determining if an ELL has possible learning disabilities?**
    (Rigorous)

    A. Observation and interpretation
    B. A language diagnostic test
    C. Documentation of at least 1 intervention
    D. Consultation with the principal about ELL's progress

Answer: A. Observation and interpretation
Answers B, C, and D are all good steps in the evaluation process. However, A is the correct selection since it is still the most commonly used tool available to educators. Unfortunately, to date, tools to determine whether a difficulty is the result of a second language learning difficulty or a learning disability are not currently available so the observations and interpretations of discerning educators are important.

88. **Which of the following is an example of distortion in pronunciation?**
    (Rigorous)

    A. Pronouncing lake as cake
    B. Pronouncing ship as chip
    C. Pronouncing liked as like-id
    D. Dropping of the final consonants of words

Answer: B. Pronouncing ship as chip
Answer A is an example of substitution, Answer C is an example of addition, Answer D is an example of omission, and Answer B is an example of distortion. Answer B is the correct choice.

89. **An ELL suspected of being gifted might demonstrate which of the following behaviors?**
    (Rigorous)

    A. May present behavioral problems when asked to produce written work
    B. Has the ability to decode successfully but difficulty in comprehensions
    C. Should be analyzed for up to 10 weeks using ESOL techniques
    D. May demonstrate the ability to solve problems not dependent on English

Answer: D. May demonstrate the ability to solve problems not dependent on English
Answer A suggests the ELL may be acting out to avoid producing work that is challenging or too difficult. Answer B is indicative of learning difficulties. Answer C indicates a procedure to avoid placing an ELL in the incorrect environment, such as a learning disabilities situation. Answer D indicates ability beyond the realm of language-learning difficulties; it suggests gifted exceptionalities. Answer D is the correct option.

90. **Which one of the following features is *not* a key feature of group learning projects?**
    (Average)

    A. Ability groups for regular daily tasks
    B. Monitoring group work during the task
    C. Assessing both individual and group achievements
    D. Meaningful tasks

Answer: A. Ability groups for regular daily tasks
Options B, C, and D are all key features of group learning projects. Only Option A has negative effects on students and is not recommended. The correct choice is A.

91. **When the teacher is correcting a student's language, the teacher should:**
    (Easy)

    A. Carefully correct all mistakes
    B. Consider the context of the error
    C. Ignore the error and increase correct input
    D. Correct only those errors that interfere with meaning

Answer: D. Correct only those errors that interfere with meaning
To carefully correct all mistakes a student makes (A) would raise the affective filter and probably cause the student to hesitate before speaking. Considering the context of the error (B) gives the teacher insight into the student's learning, but isn't a method of correction. Option C is based on Krashen's Monitor Theory and suggests that errors can be totally ignored. The best option is D, which corrects errors by suggesting more information or a correct grammar structure that will show the student the correct form and clarify meaning.

92. **Which one of the following is a purpose of feedback?**
    (Rigorous)

    A. To model structures correctly
    B. To correct mistakes
    C. To illustrate alternative forms of speech
    D. To provide assessment and correction

Answer: D. To provide assessment and correction
Answers A, B, and C are ways in which the instructor can provide scaffolding for the ELL. Answer D is the correct choice. To provide assessment and correction are the twin purposes of feedback.

93. **Which of the following strategies will help develop vocabulary in a non-threatening way?**
    (Rigorous)

    A. Menus from local restaurants
    B. Word lists for the upcoming readings
    C. Activate prior knowledge about the content, especially vocabulary
    D. Explicit instruction in the content vocabulary

Answer: A. Menus from local restaurants
Options B, C, and D are all necessary teaching strategies. However, since the emphasis is on learning new material and content, students may feel threatened. Option A is a nonthreatening way to introduce new vocabulary to students in the classroom. Option A is the correct answer.

94. **Which of the following activities is the most effective in learning to self-edit a written text?**
    (Rigorous)

    A. Checking the text for spelling errors
    B. Checking the text for grammatical errors
    C. Using a checklist provided by the teacher
    D. Revising word order

Answer: C. Using a checklist provided by the teacher
Asking most ELLs to review their work for possible errors is wasted effort—just as it would be for native speakers. Students must be trained in what to look for. Option C is the best choice since it guides the ELLs in what specific mistakes they should look for. The checklist can be drawn up to emphasis the syntactic or semantic points being emphasized in the writing exercise.

95. **Which of the following tests is used to evaluate foreign students entering the university?**
    (Rigorous)

    A. CELDT
    B. BEAR
    C. Iowa Test of Basic Skills
    D. TOEFL

Answer: D. TOEFL
Option A is the California English Language Development Test given to students to determine their program placement based upon their language skills. Option B is a commercial reading test (Basic Early Assessment of Reading) by Riverside. Option C tests basic language arts skills. Option D, the Test of English as a Foreign Language by the Educational Testing Service (ETS), is a language proficiency test. Option D would be the correct choice.

96. **Which of the following provides extra help to disadvantaged students in math and reading?**
    (Rigorous)

    A. No Child Left Behind
    B. The Dream Act
    C. Race to the Top
    D. Title I

Answer: D. Title I
The goal of Option A is to have every student proficient in reading and math by 2014. Options B is legislation stalled in Congress that would legalize certain students who were born in the U.S. or came here at an early age and attend high school but are undocumented. Option C is legislation which allows states to compete for funds by applying stricter measures to teacher accountability and school evaluation. Option D is a goal of Title I; it is the best choice.

97. Which one of the following is *not* an alternative assessment strategy used to back up oral placement testing results?
    (Rigorous)

    A. Teacher observation
    B. Conferencing
    C. Oral interviews
    D. Interviews

Answer: A. Teacher observation
Answer D is used to evaluate the student's ability to respond to simple responses based on a structured interview where the primary goal is to gauge the English level of the ELL. Answer C Oral interviews allow the teacher to evaluate the language an ELL is using and their ability to supply content information. Answer B is used by teachers to evaluate a student's improvement or decline. In conferencing, students may also learn self-evaluation techniques. Answer A allows the teacher to observe behavior and outcomes during individual or group activities. It is not necessarily used to evaluate oral performance. Answer A is the best choice.

98. Which of the following alternative assessment strategies is used to promote an inner dialogue for ELLs?
    (Average)

    A. Portfolios
    B. Observation
    C. Self-assessment
    D. Journals

Answer: D. Journals
Portfolios are a way for the work record of the student to be preserved over a period of time and can function as an assessment. Self-assessment provides the student with a way to think about their learning themselves. Answer D is the correct response since journal writing is a way ELLs can keep records and question themselves about many issues including their progress in language learning.

99. **Which of the following accommodations may be allowed for ELLs with less than one year in the Target Language environment during assessment?**
(Average)

   A. Read specific parts of the test as appropriate
   B. Paraphrasing the prompt
   C. Pronouncing vocabulary words
   D. Translating parts of the test

Answer: A. Read specific parts of the test as appropriate
Answers B, C, and D would defeat the purpose of assessing the ELLs. Answer A is the appropriate accommodation during assessment except for vocabulary or reading comprehension sections of the test.

100. **Which of the following is an acceptable teaching practice when preparing exceptional students to take tests?**
(Rigorous)

   A. Give practice timed tests
   B. Research topics extensively
   C. Teach additional vocabulary
   D. Write practice essays

Answer: A. Give practice timed tests
Answers B and C are not good techniques to use with most exceptional students because of the difficulties involved in demanding content. Vocabulary is best learned in context and not from additional word lists. Answer D writing practice essays can also be frustrating for exceptional students. Answer A is the correct response because exceptional students may get frustrated with timed tests if they are not familiar with them.

101. **Which of the following is a possible sign of the gifted ELL student?**
(Average)

   A. Advanced developmental history according to parental interview
   B. Speech delayed in L2
   C. Seems to solve logic problems with difficulty
   D. Good academic performance in L1

Answer: A. Advanced developmental history according to parental interview
Answers B and C may be signs of students with disabilities. Answer B may also be a sign of L2 learners. Answer D is a characteristic of L2 learners with normal learning abilities. Gifted students show many characteristics including an advanced developmental history as a prime indicator of a student with exceptional abilities. Answer A is the best choice.

102. **Which of the following demonstrates test or norming bias?**
(Rigorous)

   A. Administer practice tests with time limits
   B. Negative attitude of the test giver
   C. Translating from L1 to L2 literally
   D. Eliminating ELLs from the school's population

Answer: D. Eliminating ELLs from the school's population
Answer A addresses cultural bias since many cultures do not time tests and ELLs may find this a difficulty since it is a norm in many U.S. testing environments. Answer B is an example of attitudinal bias. It may result in lower test results. Answer C translation bias may result when tests are translated literally and the essence of the test is lost. Answer D eliminates ELLs or different populations for the school's norming results. This "skews" the test results and does not give a true picture of the school's norms. Answer D is the best choice.

103. **If a test question asks a student about an iPod, which kind of bias may the question contain?**
(Rigorous)

   A. Cultural
   B. Attitudinal
   C. Test/Norming
   D. Translation

Answer: A. Cultural
Option B refers to the attitude of the examiner towards a certain language, dialect, or culture. Option C occurs when ELLs are excluded in the school's population when obtaining norm results. Option D concerns translation bias caused by translating literally and possibly losing the essence of the test item. Only Option A refers to the assumption that all students and cultures are familiar with the normal experiences of a middle class North American child. A is the best choice.

104. When ELLs are asked to listen to an airport announcement of flight arrivals and departures, which type of test are they being given?
(Rigorous)

   A. First generation
   B. Second generation
   C. Third generation
   D. Traditional

Answer: C. Third generation
Option A, first generation tests, are those based on the grammar-translation method of teaching. Students are set tasks such as writing an essay or answering multiple-choice questions. Second generation (B) and traditional (D) tests are the same. They are long, discrete point tests with no connection between the test items. Option C, third generation tests, are tests that set an integrated task for the test taker, such as listening for information about an arriving train (or plane). Answer C is the correct answer.

105. Differentiated instruction is characterized by:
(Easy)

   A. Different learning goals
   B. The students are placed in learning levels
   C. The gifted student is set a list of learning objectives
   D. Materials are grouped according to ability levels

Answer: A. Different learning goals
Option D may be discounted since all materials are available to all students in differentiated instruction. Option C can be eliminated since all students are allowed to pursue the learning activity as deeply as they wish. Option B may be eliminated also since established ability grouping is a demotivating factor for students. The correct selection is A where the teacher establishes learning goals for all students and allows them to pursue the content according to their interests and abilities.

106. **Which one of the following is not true of culture and cultural differences?**
    (Average)

    A. Can adversely affect second language learning
    B. Can have a positive effect on second language learning
    C. Determines the outcome of second language learning
    D. May have strong emotional influence on the ELL learner

Answer: C. Determines the outcome of second language learning
Culture and cultural differences may be addressed by the skillful ESOL teacher, but frequently teachers are unaware of all the cultures and cultural differences they are dealing with. At the same time, it may be possible to determine how the teacher's culture affects the ELL's attitude towards education, but it may well be something the young child cannot express or the adult hides for various reasons. Culture and cultural differences do not always play a positive role in the learning process; sometimes they have negative effects. Culture and cultural differences may have a strong emotional influence—either positive or negative—on the ELL learner. Answer C states the outcomes are determined by culture. While culture greatly influences language learning, it alone does not determine the outcome. Thus, C is the best option.

107. **Which one of the following is *not* an acceptable practice when working with ELLs?**
    (Rigorous)

    A. Short wait time
    B. Establishment of group work
    C. Show and tell based on different cultures
    D. Extensive reading time

Answer: A. Short wait time
Answer B, C, and D can all be discounted since they are standard practice for language arts and ESOL teachers. Answer A, the amount of time a teacher waits for an answer from her students, can be very difficult to change. Teachers may be somewhat impatient ("Let's get on with it"), lack understanding ("If they knew the answer, they would respond"), and be unaware of differences between the U.S. and other cultures. Thus, many ELLs will need more wait time than many teachers are accustomed to giving. Answer A is the correct response.

108. When Mr. Smith planned his class on plants, he brought in plants. He also provided the students with seeds, cotton, and small jars for growing the seeds. Mr. Smith is planning a lesson that is geared towards which type of learner?
(Rigorous)

    A. Tactile
    B. Auditory
    C. Kinesthetic
    D. Visual

Answer: A. Tactile
Option D visual learners would enjoy watching a PowerPoint presentation. Option B, auditory learners, would appreciate listening to lectures accompanying a PowerPoint presentation. Option C, kinesthetic learners, would need movement to learn well so this option may be discarded. Option A, tactile learners, would enjoy touching the plants and growing plants. Option A is the best choice.

109. Which of the following suggestions would *not* create a warm, culturally aware environment?
(Rigorous)

    A. The use of English only in the classroom
    B. Inviting parents to share their experiences with the class
    C. Using scaffolding judiciously
    D. Diversifying the literature/stories in the classroom

Answer: A. The use of English only in the classroom
The culturally aware teacher would embrace Option B, C, and D as welcoming gestures to a diverse classroom population. Teachers who know their students' language may judiciously use it in the classroom to demonstrate respect for and knowledge of other cultures. Strictly adhering to an English only rule can be frustrating to many ELLs, and they would probably not recognize the classroom environment as warm or welcoming, but rather threatening. Option A is the best choice.

110. **Which of the following social factors is the single most influential element in second-language learning?**
    (Average)

    A. Age
    B. Gender
    C. Social conditions
    D. Motivation

Answer: D. Motivation
Motivation whether a trait (state) or a state (instrumental) is probably the most powerful element in the acquisition of a second language. Without family or community support, the ELL may be under tremendous pressure and feel threatened by the new language. For him or her to succeed, he or she must do so at considerable personal sacrifice. Answer D is the correct choice.

111. **In Title IX, the Supreme Court ruled that:**
    (Rigorous)

    A. School districts may not continue education programs that fail to produce positive results for ELLs
    B. Sexual harassment was prohibited in any school activity on or off campus
    C. Students were denied an "equal" education
    D. Discrimination is prohibited against students and employers based on race, ethnicity, national origins, disability, or marital status

Answer: B. Sexual harassment was prohibited in any school activity on or off campus
Answer A refers to *Castaneda v Pickard* (1981). Option C refers to *Lau v Nichols* (1974). Answer D was covered in the Florida Educational Equity Act of 1984. Answer B refers to Title IX of the Education Amendments of 1972. The correct choice is Answer B.

112. **Which of the following is most appropriate when establishing quality programs for ELLs?**
    (Rigorous)

    A. Challenge students cognitively
    B. Establishing goals to accommodate all ELLs
    C. Students are encouraged to use their native language
    D. Students need to work independently on L2 goals

Answer: A. Challenge students cognitively

Option B is incorrect since it implies lowering the standards to accommodate some ELLs. Option C is frowned upon in many schools for fear that L2 learning will be delayed. As long as no punitive action is taken against students for using their native language, students may be permitted to use L2 in the classroom. Option D is a poor choice since extensive research shows students perform better in cooperative learning situations. Option A is the best choice as all students should be challenged to use their highest abilities.

113. **The American Recovery and Reinvestment Act (2009) established:**
    (Rigorous)

    A. Title I
    B. No Child Left Behind Act (NCLB)
    C. That all students must be proficient in math and reading by 2014
    D. Race to the Top (RTT)

Answer: D. Race to the Top (RTT)

Option A refers to the establishment of voluntary school participation in NAEP after the National Committee on Excellence in Education produced their report *A Nation at Risk* (1983). The NCLB Act (Option B) was signed into law in 2002. One provision of the NCLB Act is C—all students must be proficient in math and reading by 2014. The RTT is a program included in the American Recovery and Reinvestment Act. RTT is used as a stimulus to states to improve their schools in order to earn special funds for education. Option D is the best choice.

114. The No Child Left Behind Act requires schools to:
(Rigorous)

    A. Include LEPs in some academic assessments
    B. Evaluate LEPs in their native language when possible
    C. Measure LEPs in math and reading once a year in grades 9-12
    D. Show adequate yearly progress

Answer: D. Show adequate yearly progress
Answer A is incorrect since LEPs must be included in all academic assessments. Answer B is incorrect because LEPs must be evaluated in the language most likely to provide accurate data. Answer C is incorrect because all students must be measured once a year in grades 3-8 in math and reading. Since NCLB requires schools to focus on quality education for students who were often overlooked by the educational system, in general, every public school must show adequate yearly progress (AYP) for each of the following categories: economically disadvantaged students, students from major racial and ethnic groups, students with disabilities, and students with limited English proficiency (LEP). Answer D is the correct option.

115. Which of the following is *not* a factor of the affective domain that affects language learning?
(Average)

    A. Age
    B. Anxiety
    C. Teacher expectations
    D. Scaffolding

Answer: B. Anxiety
All of the options affect language learning. Only Option B is an element of the affective filter and the correct choice.

116. Which one of the following is *not* an affective domain component?
    (Rigorous)

    A. Teacher's expectations
    B. Classroom culture
    C. Language transfer
    D. Motivation

Answer: C. Language transfer
The affective filter refers to the full range of human feelings and emotions that come into play during second-language acquisition. Learning a second language may make the learner vulnerable because he or she may have to leave his or her comfort zone behind. This can be especially difficult for adults who are used to being "powerful" or "in control" in their profession, but also affects children and teens. Answers A, B, and D are all components of the affective domain. Option C is the best selection here since language transfer from the first language may be helpful or not depending on what elements are being transferred.

117. Which of the following activities would contribute to an effective classroom culture for ELLs?
    (Rigorous)

    A. Choosing the way in which to present a book report
    B. Working individually on a project
    C. Ambiguous behavioral standards
    D. Fear of classmate's ridicule

Answer: A. Choosing the way in which to present a book reports
Students may be afraid of speaking before their classmates who might ridicule them (D). Option C is a poor teaching practice for all students because students should understand clearly what educational behaviors are expected of them. Option B working individually on projects can lead to the separation of native speakers and non-native speakers in the classroom. Integrated groups will help both groups learn to respect and to help each other with difficult assignments. Choosing the way in which to present a book report is one small choice teachers can allow students to make over their assignments. Option A is the best choice.

118. **Which of the following activities would make transitioning from high school to the workplace easier for students?**
    (Rigorous)

    A. Visiting the new campus
    B. Holding a Q-and-A session for parents
    C. Visiting with the freshman principal or dean
    D. Talking with former students in a Q-and-A session

Answer: D. Talking with former students in a Q-and-A session
Options A, B, and C are all recommended practices to ease the transition worries when students are involved in transfer between different schools, including college. Many students already have jobs by the time they are in high school. However, many don't. Option D is effective because the former students know what factors concern young adults for whom the workplace represents a new and unknown venue. Option D is the best choice.

119. **Which of the following offices would welcome parents who wish to get involved in their children's education?**
    (Average)

    A. Youth and family services
    B. TESOL
    C. AAC
    D. NABE

Answer: C. AAC
Option A is a government agency whose mission is to intervene in domestic disputes and protect children at risk (and other family members). Option B is a professional organization of teachers of English to speakers of other languages. Option D is another professional organization—the National Association of Bilingual Education. Option C is the Autism Advisory Committee and welcomes parental involvement. Option C is the best option.

120. Which of the following sources would be the most appropriate to recommend to ELLs for supplementary practice?
(Rigorous)

   A. http://www2.ed.gov/about/offices/list/ies/index.html?src=oc
   B. http://www.ed.gov/offices/OCR
   C. http://www.eslcafe.com
   D. http://www.ed.gov

Answer: C. http://www.eslcafe.com
Option A is the web address of the United States Department of Education, Office of English Language Acquisition (OELA). Option B is the web address of the Office for Civil Rights (OCR). Option D is the web address of the U. S. Department of Education. Option C Dave's ESL Café is one of the longest running websites with sections for students, teachers, and jobs. Option C is the best choice.

www.ingramcontent.com/pod-product-compliance
Lightning Source LLC
LaVergne TN
LVHW061315060426
835507LV00019B/2164